To my husband, Joe and daughter, Bianca. I love you more than you know. To my two French Bulldogs, Bernie and Brutus, who brighten up my day. To my students, who have inspired me to write with a purpose. You all mean the world to me.

-PD

Life with Lia

Lia's First Lesson

Written by Paula A. DiVincenzo

Illustrated by Ros Webb

A Message to Parents...

As a teacher, I understand the importance of children and families reading and learning together. As you travel along Lia's journey, take time to discuss the plot elements of the story with your child. When you spot a "cut-out,"

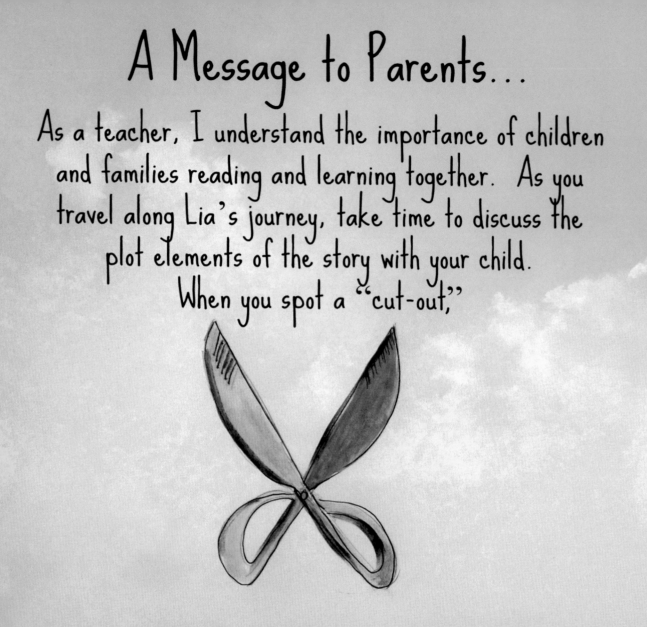

take a moment to pause and have a chat, or complete a task, to help enhance the comprehension and lessons that develop throughout "Life with Lia!"

"Wake up, Lia! It's your first day of kindergarten! Don't you want to get to school early to meet your teacher and all of your new friends?"

"I'm scared, Mommy. What if they don't like me?" Lia replied.

"Oh, Lia. School is wonderful! You are going to love Mrs. Johnson and all of the new friends you are going to make. Remember what Nonna always says?"

"You won't know until you try?"

"That's right. So, let's get up on the count of three. Ready? **ONE, TWO, THREE**!" Mommy lifted Lia into the air and spun her around. Mommy always had a way of making something scary, not so scary anymore.

Think of a time you felt scared like Lia. What feelings did you have? Were you sad, scared, mad? Who helped you? Your mom, dad, brother, sister? What did you do to get over your feeling of being scared? Did you meet a friend, go play outside, read a book? Have a chat with anyone you choose (that includes the person you are reading with!). Discuss the feelings you had, the people that were involved, and what you did to overcome your feeling of being scared. Maybe you wrote your feelings down. That would count as "feelings" and activities that helped". Maybe talking to a friend helped you – that would count as "people", "feelings" and "activities that helped"! Now that you've got it, give it a try!

Lia's tummy rumbled like rolling thunder all the way to school that day. Mommy felt that Lia was very nervous, so she took her by the hand and walked her into the BIG, red brick school building, with the BIG, red door.

As Lia entered her new classroom, she immediately noticed the smiling woman, with the dark, curly hair and colorful eyeglasses. *This must be my teacher*, Lia thought to herself. "Lia, it is so wonderful to meet you! My name is Mrs. Johnson. We are all pleased to have you join us today."

As soon as her mother left, Lia noticed a girl with long pigtails sitting by herself, in a red chair, in the corner of the room. *She looks sad*, Lia thought to herself. *Maybe she wouldn't mind if I sat next to her?*

"Hi," Lia said softly to the girl. "My name is Lia. What's your name?"

"Samantha," the girl replied with her head down.

"Can I sit next to you?" Lia asked kindly.

"Okay. I like your pink dress!"

Lia smiled. "Me, too! I picked it out myself! I like your dress, too. Purple is my other favorite color!"

Suddenly, Lia noticed a pair of eyes staring at her from across the room.

Use the lines below to make a prediction.
Who do you think was staring at
Lia from across the room?

_____

- -

_____

_____

- -

_____

Just then, Lia felt the urge to run as the group of children from across the room slowly approached her. It wasn't long before one of the boys, wearing a red and blue striped shirt, asked Lia, "Do you want to play with us?"

Lia replied excitedly, "Sure! Can Samantha come, too?"

"Not if you want to be friends with us!" exclaimed the boy in the red and blue striped shirt. The whole group of children broke out in laughter, except for Lia and Samantha.

What would you do if you were Lia?

- - - - - - - - - - - - - - -
_____

_____
- - - - - - - - - - - - - - -
_____
- - - - - - - - - - - - - - -
_____

?

Just then, Mrs. Johnson announced, "Okay, boys and girls, recess is over, time to clean up! Let's get ready for math!"

At that moment, all of the boys and girls took part in the clean up song. "Clean up, clean up, everybody do your share. Clean up, clean up, everybody, everywhere!"

One of Lia's favorite things to do in school is to trace her name. With your finger, can you help her using the letters below ?

Ring, ring! Lia couldn't have been happier to hear the sound of the dismissal bell. The first day of kindergarten was not what Lia expected, but happy to have made some friends. However, she couldn't help but think of Samantha, as she walked over to her mom who was waiting near the GIANT maple tree, in front of the school, to pick her up.

"Hi, sweetie! Can't wait to hear all about your first day!" Mommy exclaimed loudly.

Lia couldn't help but walk with her head down, as they made their way to Mommy's green minivan. Mommy knew immediately that something was troubling her. "What's wrong, honey? Everything okay? Did something happen at school?"

"Well, kinda…", Lia solemnly replied. "I met a friend….," she began.

"That's great! So what's wrong with meeting friends?"

"The other boys and girls weren't so nice to her and it made me feel bad. I wanted to help her, but I didn't know how."

"Do you remember what Nonna always says?"

"That it's better to have one real friend than a million untrue friends?"

"You betcha! And those are words to live by, my sweet pea. Come on, let's get home. I'll make your favorite snack – milk and Double Stuffed Oreos!"

Although Lia still felt bad about what happened at school, milk and Double Stuffed Oreos would maybe help a bit.

What might happen at school tomorrow?

_____

— — — — — — — — — — —

_____

_____

— — — — — — — — — — —

_____

The next day at school, Lia couldn't help the butterflies fluttering around in her tummy. *This school stuff is really tough*, she thought to herself. Why can't everyone just be friends?

Then, the sound of Mrs. Johnson's voice stopped all of the boys and girls in their tracks. "Okay, kiddies, time for recess! It's a beautiful sunny day, so we will be outside today!"

The class roared with cheers of excitement, as all the boys and girls rushed to the BIG, red door towards the back of the classroom.

As soon as Lia stepped outside, she couldn't help but notice Jimmy and Mikey, the two mean boys from yesterday, along with Gina and Emily. Gina was pretty, Lia thought, with her two, long dutch braids, stretching down the middle of her back. She always wore the *coolest* clothes, too. Today, she had on the shiniest Converse high-tops Lia had ever seen – pink sparkles and silver gems! Emily, on the other hand, was still hip, but more of a tomboy. She always wore her long hair straight, with an oversized pink Yankees baseball cap.

Suddenly, Lia realized that the whole group was staring in her direction "Hey, Lia, want to jump in a game of kickball with us?" Mikey screamed from the opposite end of the field. Lia glanced to her left-hand side where Samantha was standing. She feared, at that moment, that only one of them was invited and the other would be left out.

"No, thanks, guys. If we can't all be friends and play together, then I'm out." Lia glanced back towards Samantha who had a sheepish grin on her face. This made Lia smile in return.

As the two friends left the playground hand-in-hand, skipping and laughing without a care in the world, Lia remembered what Nonna always says, *"We must do what's in our heart to help us make the choices that are right for us and the ones we love"*.

Lia decided, from that day forward, she would never forget Nonna's message and the lessons she learned in kindergarten that school year.

Did you ever have to make a choice you knew wasn't popular, like Lia's, but you knew it was the right thing to do? Explain

_____

- -

_____

_____

- -

_____